The Battle
Of
Maldon

Johnny:
Hope you enjoy!
It was a labor of
love.
regards,

[signature]

8/12/96

By the Same Author

SONGS FROM THE SEA
NOAH'S ARK

THE BATTLE
OF
MALDON

Translated and Introduced by
SAMUEL SALERNO

LIGHTHOUSE PRESS   *   MONTEREY, CA

Printed in the United States of America

ISBN 0-9638322-0-0

Cover Illustration and Map by Katy Moore

For
Steve, Sean, Alex,
and
the Boys:

Mood the More...

CONTENTS

ACKNOWLEDGMENTS

With gratitude, I would like to acknowledge Brenda Stockdale for her assistance in editing the manuscript. I am also indebted to Dr. Frederic Roth for his helpful suggestions regarding the introduction, and to Katy Moore and D.R. Parker for their unswerving moral and technical support. Finally, my thanks to Dr. Loftur Bjarnason whose example and inspiration permeate this work, though he is not here to see its completion.

INTRODUCTION

I.

The year is A.D. 991, and the Danes are on the move. Fresh from a stabilizing period of rule over the North Sea region, restless Viking warriors are pushing out to sea in their long ships, in search of glory and plunder-- the quiet coasts of eastern Britain directly in their path. Heading west the gritty Norsemen are merciless in their attacks against the Isles, sailing up waterways and through inland rivers, bringing to the heartlands of Saxon England yet another reign of terror.

Although the Danish presence in the British Isles had already been established as early as the first half of the ninth century, the English had enjoyed a period of relative peace in the quarter century leading up to the renewed Danish incursions, beginning around A.D. 980. With the resumption of the " Viking fury", a new and losing struggle ensued in which two grim choices became apparent for the embattled Saxons: pay tribute or die fighting.

So begins our story: the tale of the Battle of Maldon, a bloody engagement in 991 between Norse raiders and their English opponents led by the Saxon thane, Byrhtnoth. From the *Anglo-Saxon Chronicle* we read:

In this year (991) Anlaf came with ninety-three ships to Folkestone and ravaged the neighborhood... and so to Maldon. And there Ealdorman Byrhtnoth and his fyrd came to meet him and fought with him. And they killed the Ealdorman and the battle field was theirs.[1]

11

In another version, from the 12th century, the *Liber Eliensis* states:

> The Vikings had sent word to him (Byrhtnoth) that they had come to avenge their countrymen... Byrhtnoth, inflamed to a pitch of daring by this message, summoned his former companions in arms, and with a few men at arms marched off to give battle.[2]

We are give a fuller account of the battle of Maldon in the poem of the same name, written anonymously after the conflict.

II.

The town of Maldon is located on the southeast coast of England, some twenty-five miles below Ipswich, in Essex. Maldon sits at the end of an inlet opposite Northey Island and above the Blackwater Estuary. It is generally assumed that the actual battle site was situated below Maldon in the estuary. At that location, Northey Island is connected to the mainland by a causeway approximately two hundred and forty yards long and eighty feet wide (though this distance was more than likely much shorter at the time of the engagement). [3] Strategically, it makes sense that the Viking force would land its ships at Northey rather than sailing farther up river and prompting the potential cut-off of a necessary retreat. The causeway itself is only passable at low tide, and it is thought that the men of Essex were situated on the side opposite that of the Viking force's position. Though the causeway was bridgeable, the Norsemen were well within range of Saxon spears, and were thus beset with the problem of finding a safe way across in order to give battle. Passage was finally granted by the Saxon commander Byrhtnoth, as recounted in the poem:

> "Now your way is clear; come quickly to us,
> Men to arms! God alone knows
> Who will win the field this day."
> (93-95)

In the subsequent fight, Byrhtnoth is killed, and many of his companions flee the battlefield. A few of his men, hopelessly outnumbered, remain to fight to the death, in order that "they might avenge their kind lord/ and deal death to their foes."[4]

Much has been made of Byrhtnoth's decision to allow the Vikings to cross the causeway. As the poem recounts, The Danish force was allowed access due to Byrhtnoth's "Battle-pride" (line 89); what Irving (1961) has characterized as an "example of stupidity" (462). The word in Old English is *ofermode*, literally translated as "pride". The word *ofermode* appears to suggest a rashness or vainglorious attitude on the part of the Saxon thane (a tragic flaw?); however, I have chosen to translate the word as "battle-pride" for two reasons: first, and of less importance, the compound noun "battle-pride" preserves the syllabic content of the original word, and keeps the alliterative quality of the line (e.g.. battle, began); Second, is the setting in which the word is used. As Ute Schwab (1993) points out, "What would have happened if the Ealdorman Byrhtnoth had *not* asked the Danes to cross over where his army already stood waiting for them? Obviously, neither victory nor defeat"(73). It is probable, as Griffiths (1991) suggests, that the Viking force simply could have picked up and left to pillage elsewhere (81). It is plausible-- and certainly reinforced within the context of a warrior society-- that Byrhtnoth's "ofermode" was less rash arrogance than a choice based on a sense of propriety (or honor). Indeed, it is doubtful that the demands of leading men in the defense of their homeland, along with the comprehension of the earnest spirit of warfare that characterized the age, would have been lost to the thane's decision-making process. "Battle-pride", then, implies a calculated emotional response within the parameters of a potential fight.

III.

No one knows who wrote *The Battle of Maldon*. The manuscript containing the poem was destroyed in a library fire in 1731. Fortunately, a copy of the poem was rendered some years prior to the fire, though segments are missing (i.e. the beginning and end of the poem). Thus, the 325 lines that come to us in the present form are of a fragmentary nature. Linguistic evidence suggests that the poem was written sometime within a period of two decades after the battle. [6]   As to the author, a few (Alexander 1991, et al.) Have suggested that the poet may have been a participant in the engagement (99). A more likely possibility is that the poem had its origins in the ecclesiastical tapestry of the day, and that a monk from a nearby Abbey penned the verse. [7] The recording of memorable events-- such as the death of a prominent nobleman in battle-- was not an uncommon occurrence in monastic circles of the era. The author, or ecclesiastics in general, may well have been able to provide relatively accurate accounts of battle formations and other acts of stratagem. [8] Further, The Maldon account of the desperate last stand of the loyal Saxons may be construed as a solemn attempt to recall an earlier day in which the Germanic warrior code (or comitatus) held sway (i.e. that heroes stay on the field with their fallen lord rather than retreat in shame). [9] In such a case, the poet functions as intermediary between ethic and act-- the warrior-priest who both confirms and perpetuates the heroic ideal in poem and song.

Whether *Maldon* was written as contemporary social commentary for a beleaguered island people, as an extended elegy, or simply as an historical record may never be fully resolved. Nevertheless, each premise is provocative. [10] It may be sufficient to say that the poem encompasses elements of all three objectives. This incomplete piece from a nearly forgotten age certainly inspires, laments, and records the passing of a noted figure of Saxon times.

What is clear is the poet's sometimes plaintive tone, first realized in the bittersweet, though resolute final speeches of the Saxon warriors who stay behind (lines 202-324), and most acutely sounded in the final admonition of the poem:

Næs þæt nā se Godrīc̆ þe þā gūðe forbēah!

(325)

Of perhaps equal power and emotion are the words uttered by Byrhtwold, an old warrior whose time is limited:

"Hiġe sceal þē heardra, heorte þē cēnre,
mōd sceal þē māre þē ūre mæġen lytlað."

(312-313)

At the end, the Maldon poet displays a remarkable affinity for-- and intimacy towards- the men who fought and died in the battle. As the generally dispassionate narrative lapses into a brooding pitch a dying heroic ideal is recalled, along with the uncertainty of the fate of a once united people.

IV.

The Battle of Maldon is not well known outside of literary circles. Overshadowed by the Southern pre-eminence in the literature of antiquity, Old English literature, with the notable exception of *Beowulf*, has often been relegated to a minor position in both Western letters and the Western psyche. Fortunately, this long established tendency has gradually been modified towards a more inclusive paradigm: one in which the ornate beauty of Southern European literature is not " bruised to pleasure" the haunting and iron echoes of the ancient Northern traditions. It is within the context of a need to celebrate our literary and linguistic heritage, and of the timeless nature of Maldon's message, that I have chosen to present a translation of this relatively obscure work.

Though it is apparent that the cultural connotations once wed to words divorce themselves over the vast distances of time, it should not therefore be assumed that we must lose all semblance of the beauty that informed the resonance of the language in question. It is heartening to recall from time to time (as with *Maldon*) that in a violent age of perpetual warfare pause was given to capture the enduring spirit of a people and their language. This, true of today, is certainly the translator's most difficult, yet most desirous, task. Any attempt to re-introduce an unfamiliar work is a "leap of faith"-- a tentative pact between the elusive cultures and tongues of two very different ages. The translator, then, is entrusted with the charge of becoming a bridge between two peoples whose hopes and fears and history are realized in the art of their languages.

And how more compelling, paradoxically, is Maldon's certain relevance to the individual and collective lives of those who have endured the twentieth century. In an age of unprecedented carnage and savagery (in terms of the high technology of mass destruction and sheer body-count), we have faced the fatalism of a century without God; an uncertain age of crumbling spiritual architectures in which a cacophony of cultures and philosophies "clash by night"; an age in which human destiny is not so much determined by the values of custom and ceremony, but by the consequences of individual choice-- our own acts of bravery or cowardice. Even now, one thousand years later, *The Battle of Maldon* speaks its truths with greater urgency.

Ultimately, a work of art must speak first to the individual and then, hopefully, to the community at large. It is with this in mind that *The Battle of Maldon* should be read. Here then is a lasting testament, spoken from across the ages, to friendship, cowardice, and to the indomitable spirit of man in the face of his living and death.

SS-1996

PRONUNCIATION

a	as the first vowel in 'aha'
ā	long vowel as in 'call'
æ	short as in 'chatter'/long as in 'land'
c	as in 'can'
ċ	as in 'chin'
cg	as 'dj'(ex: edge)
e	as in 'met'
ē	as in 'late' (akin to German 'Sehen')
f	as in 'fit'/ between vowels as 'v'
g	as in 'god'
ġ	as 'y' in 'yell'
ī	long as in 'keen'
o	as in 'fought'
ō	as in 'so'
u	as in 'pull'
ū	as in 'fool'
y	lips together as in French 'tu'
sc	as 'sh' (ex: ship)
þ	voiced or voiceless 'th' (ex: paths/path)
ð	also 'th' (voiced between vowels, as is þ)

The long 'æ' and 'y' are not noted in the text. In addition, punctuation was not a feature of Old English texts, though it is provided here. For pronunciation and punctuation I have relied primarily on Griffiths (1991) and Mitchell & Robinson (1992).

THE BATTLE
OF
MALDON

I. The Gathering

...brocen wurde
Hēt þā hysse hwæne hors forlætan,
feor āfysan and forð gangan,
hicgan tō handum and tō hiġe gōdum.

5 Þā þæt Offan mæġ ærest onfunde
þæt se eorl nolde yrhðo ġeþolian,
hē lēt him þā of handon lēofne flēogan
hafoc wið þæs holtes, and tō þære hilde stōp;
be þām man mihte oncnāwan þæt se cniht nolde

10 wācian æt þām wīġe þā hē tō wæpnum fēng.
Ēac him wolde Ēadrīċ his ealdre ġelæstan,
frēan tō ġefeohte: ongan þā forð beran
gār tō gūþe - hē hæfde gōd ġeþanc
þā hwīle þe hē mid handum healdan mihte

15 bord and brād swurd; bēot hē ġelæste
þa hē ætforan his frēan feohtan sceolde.
Đā þær Byrhtnōð ongan beornas trymian:
rād and rædde, rincum tæhte
hū hī sceoldon standan and þone stede healdan,

20 and bæd þæt hyra randan rihte hēoldon
fæste mid folman, and ne forhtedon nā.
Þā hē hæfde þæt folc fæġere ġetrymmed,
hē līhte þā mid lēodon þær him lēofost wæs
þær hē his heorðwerod holdost wiste.

I. The Gathering

The column was halted...
He ordered the men each from his horse,
to drive them off and move forward to fight;
hearken to hands and noble hearts.
5   When Offa's kinsman once understood
that the earl would have no cowardice
he let then from hands his beloved fly,
his hawk to the woods, and ready advanced
so that all would see that this youth was not
10   to waver in battle when he took to his weapons.
Like him, Eadric longed to serve his lord
with boldness in battle, and brought forward
his spear to sing- and he gave special thanks
for the time his hands could hold to
15   shield and broadsword- a vow he made good
when in front of his lord he came to fight.
At once Byrhtnoth began to form his force.
He rode round, directed defenders
on how they must stand and hold strong,
20   and bade them bear their shields true,
firm with fist and without fear.
When all his forces were properly fixed
he dismounted among those dear friends,
the men he knew most loyal to their lord.

II. Challenges are made

Þā stōd on stæðe, stīðlīċe clypode
Wīcinga ār, wordum mælde.
Sē on bēot ābēad brimlīþendra
ærænde tō þām eorle þær hē on ōfre stōd:
"Mē sendon tō þē sæmen snelle,
30 hēton ðē secgan þæt þū mōst sendan raðe
bēagas wið ġebeorge, and ēow betere is
þæt ġē þisne gārræs mid gafole forġyldon
þon wē swā hearde hilde dælon.
Ne þurfe wē ūs spillan ġif ġē spēdaþ tō þām:
35 wē willað wið þām golde grið fæstinian;
ġyf þū þat ġerædest, þe hēr rīcost eart,
þæt þū þīne lēoda lysan wille,
syllan sæmannum on hyra sylfra dōm
fēoh wið frēode and niman frið æt ūs,
40 wē willaþ mid þām sceattum ūs tō scype gangan,
on flot fēran and ēow friþes healdan."
Byrhtnōð maþelode, bord hafenode,
wand wācne æsc, wordum mælde,
yrre and ānræd āġeaf him andsware:
45 "Gehyrst þū sælida, hwæt þis folc seġeð?
Hī willað ēow tō gafole gāras syllan,
ættrynne ord and ealde swurd,
þā hereġeatu þe ēow æt hilde ne dēah!
Brimmanna boda, ābēod eft onġēan,
50 seġe þīnum lēodum miccle lāþre spell,
þæt hēr stynt unforcūð eorl mid his werode
þe wile ġealgean ēþel þysne,

22

II. Challenges are made

25 Then standing on the shore and sternly calling out
the Vikings' herald hailed him,
boasting, and with all speed bid the oarsmen's
message to the earl who stood opposite :
Bold seamen send me to you;
30 command me to say that you quickly send
gold for fair fortune, for better it be
you buy your way from battle now
than we thus deal you death.
Nay, there's no need for blood be you rich enough.
35 We will with such gold grant a truce
if you decide who holds this day-
pay for the safety of your people-
Then give us oarsmen of our own accord
proper payment, and accepting peace from us
40 we'll take this gold, board our ships, and go-
we'll set our sails to sea and trouble you no more."
Byrhtnoth began to speak, with board-shield aloft;
he shook his slender spear, his war-words
hot and resolute- he gave his retort:
45 "Hear you, seafarer, what these men say?
They wish to give you spears for gold,
deadly axe and certain steel-
This will be the tribute you can try to win.
Danish mouthpiece, deliver this reply.
50 Tell your men a much crueler tale,
that here stands untarnished an earl with his troops
who will defend this domain,

Æþelredes eard, ealdres mīnes
folc and foldan. Feallan sceolon
55 hæþene æt hilde! Tō hēanliċ mē þinċeð
þæt ġē mid ūrum sceattum tō scype gangon
unbefohtene nū ġē þus feor hider
on ūrne eard in becōmon;
ne sceole ġe swā sōfte sinċ ġegangan:
60 ūs sceal ord and ecg ær ġesēman,
grim gūðplega, ær wē gofol syllon!"

III. Crossing the ford

Hēt þā bord beran, beornas gangan
þæt hī on þām ēasteðe ealle stōdon.
Ne mihte þær for wætere werod tō þām ōðrum
65 þær cōm flōwende flōd æfter ebban;
lucon lagustrēamas; tō lang hit him þūhte
hwænne hī tōgædere gāras bēron.
Hī þær Pantan strēam mid prasse bestōdon,
Ēastseaxena ord and se æschere;
70 ne mihte hyra æniġ ōþrum derian
būton hwā þurh flānes flyht fyl ġenāme.
Se flōd ūt ġewāt- þā flotan stōdon ġearowe,
Wīcinga fela, wīġes ġeorne.
Hēt þā hæleða hlēo healdan þā bricge
75 wigan wīġheardne sē wæs hāten Wulfstān,
cāfne mid his cynne; þæt wæs Cēolan sunu
þe ðone forman man mid his francan ofscēat
þe þær baldlīcost on þā bricge stōp.
Þær stōdon mid Wulfstāne wigan unforhte,
80 Ælfere and Maccus, mōdiġe twēġen,

Æthelred's lands, my lord's
family and fields. This fight to come
55 you heathens will find it hard! T'would be a shame
to turn back with our tribute
without a fight, having thus far
into our country come.
Our silver's not so swiftly won
60 but spear and sword decide it first-
bloody battle before we give our gold!"

III. Crossing the ford

He then bade them ready shields and step forth
so that they stood on the opposite shore's edge.
Stopped by the stream each could not reach the other.
65 The forceful flood held sway;
the inlet was locked-- too long it seemed
till the armies could close ranks and clash.
They paused at the Panta, proudly arrayed:
Saxon soldiers and the army of the ash-ships.
70 Each side could not strike the other
but by arrow-fall their fates were met.
So then the stream ebbed out-- the oarsmen stood ready;
a terrible host, hot for war.
Byrhtnoth bid then a brave man hold the bridge.
75 A tested warrior, Wulfstan was his name,
courageous among his kind; He was Ceola's son
who with his lance struck down the leading man,
the one who so boldly dared his death upon the bridge.
There too stood two warriors with Wulfstan.
80 Ælfere and Maccus, both stern of mood and unafraid-

þā noldon æt þām forda flēam ġewyrcan,
ac hī fæstlīċe wið ðā fynd weredon
þā hwīle þe hī wæpna wealdan mōston.
Þā hī þæt ongēaton and ġeorne ġesāwon
þæt hī þær bricgweardas bitere fundon,
ongunnon lyteġian þā lāðe ġystas,
bædon þæt hī upgangan āgan mōston,
ofer þone ford faran, fēþan lædan.
Ðā se eorl ongan for his ofermōde
ālyfan landes tō fela lāþere ðēode;
ongan ċeallian þā ofer cald wæter
Byrhtelmes bearn; beornas ġehlyston:
"Nū ēow is ġerymed, gāð riċene tō ūs
guman tō gūþe! God āna wāt
hwā þære wælstōwe wealdan mōte."

IV. The Battle begins

Wōdon þā wælwulfas, for wætere ne murnon,
wīcinga werod, west ofer Pantan,
ofer scīr wæter scyldas wēgon,
lidmen tō lande linde bæron.
Þær ongēan gramum gearowe stōdon
Byrhtnōð mid beornum; hē mid bordum hēt
wyrcan þone wīhagan, and þæt werod healdan
fæste wið fēondum. Þā wæs feohte nēh,
tīr æt getohte. Wæs sēo tīd cumen
þæt þær fæge men feallan sceoldon.
þær wearð hrēam āhafen, hremmas wundon,
earn æses georn; wæs on eorþan cyrm.
Hī lēton þā of folman fēolhearde speru,

They would not take flight from the ford,
but firmly defend it against any foe,
so long as they could wield weapons.
When the Norsemen realized and saw ready
85   bridge guards and were bitter met,
they plied their trade of crafty words- treacherous seamen!
They pleaded for passage, possession of the landing;
to bring their foot-troops over the ford.
Then the earl, on account of his battle-pride, began
90   to let those hateful people pass.
He called out across the cold water
and the sea-lords listened to his words:
"Now your way is clear; come quickly to us,
men to arms! God alone knows
95   who will win the field this day."

IV. The Battle begins

The wolves of war advanced, careless of water;
Viking warriors streaming west
over the shining waters bearing shields--
sea-lords on land, with armor and lance.
100   They stood ready to meet the strangers,
Byrhtnoth with his host. He ordered them to take their
shields and form a battle-wall, and commanded his men
to hold fast against the foe. Now the fight was near,
glory in warfare given. The time was gain come
105   that there doomed men should die.
War-cries were raised; ravens circled,
eagles eager for food- a great clamor on the earth!
Then flew from hands file-hard spears,

grimme gegrundene   gāras flēogan;
bogan wæron bysige,   bord ord onfēng.
Biter wæs se beaduræs,   beornas fēollon
on gehwæðere hand,   hyssas lāgon.
Wund wearð Wulfmær,   wælræste gecēas,
Byrhtnōðes mæg;   hē mid billum wearð,
his swustersunu,   swīðe forhēawen.
Þær wearð wīcingum   wiþerlēan āgyfen.
Gehyrde ic þæt Ēadweard   ānne slōge
swīðe mid his swurde,   swenges ne wyrnde,
þæt him æt fōtum fēoll   fæge cempa;
þæs him his ðēoden   þanc gesæde,
þām būrþēne,   þā hē byre hæfde.
Swā stemnetton   stīðhicgende
hysas æt hilde,   hogodon georne
hwā þær mid orde   ærost mihte
on fægean men   feorh gewinnan,
wigan mid wæpnum;   wæl fēol on eorðan.
Stōdon stædefæste;   stihte hī Byrhtnōð,
bæd þæt hyssa gehwylc   hogode tō wīge
þe on Denon wolde   dōm gefeohtan.

V. The Death of Byrhtnoth

Wōd þā wīges heard,   wæpen ūp āhōf,
bord tō gebeorge,   and wið þæs beornes stōp.
Ēode swā ānræd   eorl tō þām ceorle,
ægþer hyra ōðrum   yfeles hogode.
Sende ðā se særinc   sūþerne gār,
þæt ġewundod wearð   wigena hlāford;
hē scēaf þā mid ðām scylde,   þæt se sceaft tōbærst,

28

grimly fashioned spikes to speed.
110 Bows were busy; board-shields drew spears;
bitter was the battle-storm-- brave men fell.
On either side young sons lay still.
One wounded was Wulfmær; death in war his fate.
Byrhtnoth's kinsman (his sister's son), he was
115 bloodied by blades and swiftly cut down.
Death was dealt back to the Danes.
Heard I that Eadward struck one
with savage strokes of his sword,
so that the doomed man fell dead at his feet.
120 For this his lord gave thanks to him;
praised the chamberlain when the chance arose.
Thus stood firm the strong of heart;
brave youths fought keenly to see
who first with his spear could win
125 a fated man's life-- who might fell
a warrior by his weapon. So the wounded lay dying,
and others stood steadfast. Byrhtnoth stirred them on,
bade each Saxon give thought to the fight,
whoso wished to gain glory upon the Danes.

V. The Death of Byrhtnoth

130 Went forth then battle's brave son with weapon raised,
and bearing board-shield stepped toward a soldier-
bold of mood Byrhtnoth advanced on the churl.
Each intended ill for the other.
Then the sea-goer threw a southern spear
135 . so that the warriors' lord was wounded.
But he shoved it with his shield and split the shaft

and þæt spere sprengde, þæt hit sprang ongēan.
Gegremod wearð se gūðrinc; hē mid gāre stang
wlancne wīcing, þe him þā wunde forġeaf.
140 Frōd wæs se fyrdrinċ; hē lēt his francan wadan
þurh ðæs hysses hals, hand wīsode
þæt hē on þām færsccaðan feorh ġeræhte.
Ðā hē ōþerne ofstlīce scēat,
þæt sēo byrne tōbærst; hē wæs on brēostum wund
145 þurh ðā hringlocan, him æt heortan stōd
ætterne ord. Se eorl wæs þē blīþra,
hlōh þā, mōdi man, sæde Metode þanc
ðæs dæġweorċes þe him Drihten forġeaf.
Forlēt þā drenga sum daroðof handa,
150 flēogan of folman, þæt sē tō forð gewāt
þurh ðone æþelan Æþelrēdes þegen.
Him be healfe stōd hyse unweaxen,
cniht on gecampe, se full cāflīce
bræd of þām beorne blōdigne gār,
155 Wulfstānes bearn, Wulfmær se ġeonga,
forlēt forheardne faran eft ongēan;
ord in gewōd, þæt sē on eorþan læg
þe his þēoden ær þearle ġeræhte.
Ēode þā ġesyrwed secg tō þām eorle;
160 hē wolde þæs beornas bēagas gefecgan,
rēaf and hringas and gerēnod swurd.
Þā Byrhtnōð bræd bill of scēðe,
brād and brūneccg, and on þā byrnan slōh.
Tō raþe hine gelette lidmanna sum,
165 þā hē þæs eorles earm āmyrde.
Fēoll þā tō foldan fealohilte swurd;
ne mihte hē gehealdan heardne mēce,
wæpnes wealdan. Þā ġyt þæt word gecwæð
hār hilderinc, hyssas bylde,

so the spike quivered and fell out.
The old warrior was full of wrath- with his spear he
stabbed the bold-faced Viking who drew his blood.
140 War-wise was the Saxon thane; he threw his spear
through the norseman's neck- so hand guided it-
and took from the foe his life.
Then he quickly threw another
so that the seaman's mail broke; his breast was struck
145 through the chain-steel-- stopped in his heart
the fatal lance. The earl was the happier;
the brave thane laughed loud; gave God thanks
for the day's work the lord delivered him.
Then launched some Viking a lance from hand;
150 it flew from his fingers speeding forth
toward Æthelred's noble thane.
Standing by his side a servant,
a boy in battle, bravely
drew from Byrhtnoth the bloody spear.
155 Wulfstan's son, Wulfmær the young,
let fly a spear firmly in reply,
and struck him who had wounded Wulfmær's lord
so that he fell dead on the field.
Then ventured forward a Viking to the earl
160 intent to grab the thane's gold-goods,
his raiment and rings and rich sword.
Thereupon Byrhtnoth drew his bright blade from sheath-
his broadsword- and struck the norseman's breast-plate;
but there soon another seaman stepped between
165 and swinging struck the earl's arm-
then fell the gold-hilted sword to the ground.
Now hope was lost to hold steel
or wield weapons, yet still the thane
uttered commands; he encouraged his comrades-

170   bæd gangan forð   gōde gefēran;
       ne mihte þā on fōtum leng   fæste gestandan.
       Hē tō heofenum wlāt:
       "Geþancie þē,   ðēoda Waldend,
       ealra þæra wynna   þe iċ on worulde gebād.
175   Nū ic āh, milde Metod,   mæste þearfe
       þæt þū mīnum gāste   gōdes ġeunne,
       þæt mīn sāwul tō ðē   sīðian mōte
       on þīn ġeweald,   þēoden engla,
       mid friþe ferian.   Ic eom frymdi tō þē
180   þæt hī helscēaðan   hynan ne mōton."
       Ðā hine hēowon   hæðene scealcas
       and bēgen þā beornas   þe him biġ stōdon,
       Ælfnōð and Wulmær   bēgen lāgon,
       ðā onemn hyra frēan   feorh ġesealdon.

VI. Godric flees

185   Hī bugon þā fram beaduwe   þe þær bēon noldon.
       þær wearð Oddan bearn   ærest on flēame,
       Godrīċ fram gūþe,   and þone gōdan forlēt
       þē him mænigne oft   mēarh gesealde;
       hē ġehlēop þone eoh   þe āhte his hlāford,
190   on þām ġerædum   þe hit riht ne wæs,
       and his brōðru mid him   bēġen ærndon,
       Godwine and Godwīġ,   gūþe ne gymdon,
       ac wendon fram þām wīge   and þone wudu sōhton,
       flugon on þæt fæsten   and hyra fēore burgon,
195   and manna mā   þonne hit ænig mæð wære,
       gyf hī þā ġeearnunga   ealle gemundon
       þe hē him tō duguþe   ġedōn hæfde,
       Swā him Offa on dæg   ær āsæde
       on þām meþelstede,   þā hē gemōt hæfde,

170 bade his worthy war-men go on.
No longer was he firmly afoot,
but looking to heaven the hero spoke:
"I thank thee, O ruler of nations
for the wealth of joy I given me in this world.
175 Yet now, merciful maker, I have most need
that you grant good favor to my spirit,
that my soul to thee might go,
into thy kingdom, lord of lights
in peaceful passage. I pray of you
180 that hell-fiends hath no hand with it!
Thereupon the heathens hacked him down
and both battle-men who stood with him,
Ælfnoth and Wulmær, so that they too lay dead,
fallen on the field alongside their lord.

VI. Godric flees

185 Then they fled from the battle who thought not of fight-
there went Odda's kin, the first to flight;
he was Godric who gave his good lord up-
that thane who many a mare had given him.
He leapt upon the very horse his earl had owned,
190 took those reins he was not worthy of
and his brothers with him both rode away,
Godwine and Godwig, having no blood for battle,
but turning from the fight towards the forest.
They fled to that fortress to save their lives,
195 and many more followed than it were fit
if they had all recalled the favors
their thane had done for them.
So likewise to them had Offa said on the day before
at the war-council he had called;

þæt þær mōdelīce   manega spræcon
þe eft æt þearfe   þolian noldon.

VII. The Brave stand

Þā wearð āfeallen   þæs folces ealdor,
Æþelrēdes eorl;   ealle ġesāwon
heorðgenēatas   þæt hyra heorra læg.
205 þā ðær wendon forð   wlance þeġenas,
unearge men   efston georne;
hī woldon þā ealle   ōðer twēga,
līf forlætan   oððe lēofne gewrecan.
Swā hī bylde forð   bearn Ælfrīces,
210 wiga wintrum geong, wordum mælde,
Ælfwine þā cwæð,   hē on ellen spræc:
"Gemunu þā mæla   þe wē oft æt meodo spræcon,
þonne wē on bence   bēot āhōfon,
hæleð on healle,   ymbe heard ġewinn;
215 nū mæg cunnian   hwā cēne sy.
Ic wylle mīne æþelo   eallum ġecyþan,
þæt ic wæs on Myrcon   miccles cynnes;
wæs mīn ealda fæder   Ealhelm hāten,
wīs ealdorman,   woruldġesæliġ.
220 Ne sceolon mē on þære þēode   þegenes ætwītan
þæt ic of ðisse fyrde   fēran wille,
eard ġesēcan,   nū mīn ealdor liġeð
forhēawen æt hilde.   Mē is þæt hearma mæst;
hē wæs æġðer mīn mæg   and mīn hlāford."
225 Þā hē forð ēode,   fæhðe ġemunde,
þæt hē mid orde   ānne geræhte
flotan on þām folce,   þæt sē on foldan læġ
forwēgen mid his wæpne.   Ongan þā winas manian,
frynd and ġefēran,   þæt hī forð ēodon.

34

200 That there had many made boasts
who afterwards at need would not endure.

VII. The Brave stand

So now was fallen the army's father,
Æthelred's earl. They all could see,
his hearth-friends, that their lord lay dead,
205 and those proud thanes went forth-
unflinching men- they hastened forward,
wished one of two fates:
to lay down their lives or avenge their beloved.
So they encouraged Ælfric's son to speak;
210 a warrior young in winters, spoke the words of his heart.
Ælfwine raised his voice to valor:
"Remember the times we made oaths over mead;
when we at our benches boasted,
heroes in the hall intending hard war:
215 now we will see who keeps his word!
I pray my heirs make it known
that I was among the Mercians of noble kin-
was my elder father Ealhelm called,
a wise ruler and world-wealthy.
220 None dare reproach this thane
that I should seek safety from this ford
and venture home when my lord lay
dead here on the ground. This is the greatest of griefs-
he was both my kinfolk and my king."
225 Then he went forth, his fury recalled,
and struck a sea-farer with his spear
so that the Viking fell on the field,
cut down by Ælfwine's weapon. He then began to rally
his comrades and friends so that they too advanced.

230 Offa ġemælde, æscholt āscēoc:
"Hwæt þū, Ælfwine, hafast ealle ġemanode
þegenas tō þearfe, nū ūre þēoden līð,
eorl on eorðan. Ūs is eallum þearf
þæt ūre æghwylc ōþerne bylde
235 wigan tō wīge, þā hwīle þe hē wæpen mæġe
habban and healdan, heardne mēce,
gār and gōd swurd. Ūs Godrīċ hæfð,
earh Oddan bearn, ealle beswiċene.
Wēnde þæs formoni man, þā hē mēare rād,
240 on wlancan þām wicge, þæt wære hit ūre hlāford;
forþan wearð hēr on felda folc tōtwæmed,
scyldburh tōbrocen. Ābrēoðe his angin,
þæt hē hēr swā maniġne man āflymde!"
Lēofsunu gemælde and his linde āhōf,
245 bord tō gebeorge; hē þām beorne oncwæð:
"Ic þæt gehāte, þæt iċ heonon nelle
flēon fōtes trym, ac wille furðor gān,
wrecan on ġewinne mīnne winedrihten.
Ne þurfon mē embe Stūrmere stedefæste hælæð
250 wordum ætwītan, nū mīn wine gecranc,
þæt iċ hlāfordlēas hām sīðie,
wende fram wīġe, ac mē sceal wæpen niman,
ord and īren." Hē ful yrre wōd,
feaht fæstlīce, flēam hē forhogode.
255 Dunnere þā cwæð, daroð ācwehte,
unorne ċeorl, ofer eall clypode,
bæd þæt beorna gehwylc Byrhtnōð wræce:
Ne mæġ nā wandian se þe wrecan þenceð
frēan on folċe, ne for fēore murnan."
260 Þā hī forð ēodon, fēores hī ne rōhton;

230 Offa spoke next, shaking his spear:
"Lo, you, Ælfwine, have urged us all on,
thanes to the fray. Now our lord lies dead,
fallen on the field. The need is now for us
to each encourage the other,
235 warriors to war-play, however long with weapon
he holds fast and firm; hard steel,
spear and good sword. Godric the coward,
faithless son of Odda, betrays us all!
Alack, too many thought him their master
240 as he rode off on that splendid steed,
thus is our desperate army divided
and shield-walls broken- his bearing be damned
to put proud men to flight!"
Leofsunu spoke next, raised his linden-board;
245 shook his shield and said to the warrior:
"Upon my word I will not from here
fly a foot's step, but further forward go
and avenge in battle my beloved lord.
No steadfast man round Sturmer
250 dare reproach me now that my friend is fallen-
that lordless I would leave for home;
turn away from warfare- rather I take to my weapons,
spear and fired sword!" Full of fury he advanced,
and fought with no thought of flight.
255 Dunnere then spoke, and shook his spear;
the yeoman cried out above the crowd,
bade each warrior wreak vengeance for Byrhtnoth:
"Those who desire revenge draw not back-
avenge our lord, mourn not for life lost!"
260 They then went forth, forgetting their lives.

VIII. The End

Ongunnon þā hīredmen   heardlīċe feohtan,
grame gārberend,   and God bædon
þæt hī mōston ġewrecan   hyra winedrihten
and on hyra fēondum   fyl gewyrcan.
265   Him se gysel ongan   ġeornlīċe fylstan;
hē wæs on Norðhymbron   heardes cynnes,
Ecglāfes bearn,   him wæs Æscferð nama.
Hē ne wandode nā   æt þām wīġplegan,
ac hē fysde forð   flān genehe;
270   hwīlon hē on bord scēat,   hwīlon beorn tæsde,
æfre embe stunde   hē sealde sume wunde,
þā hwīle ðe hē wæpna   wealdan mōste.
Þā ġyt on orde stōd   Ēadweard se langa,
gearo and ġeornful,   gylpwordum spræc
275   þæt hē nolde flēogan   fōtmæl landes,
ofer bæċ būgan,   þā his betera leġ.
Hē bræc þone bordweall   and wið þā beornas feaht,
oðþæt hē his sincġyfan   on þām sæmannum
wurðlīce wrec,   ær hē on wæle læġe.
280   Swā dyde Æþerīċ,   æþele gefēra,
fūs and forðġeorn,   feaht eornoste.
Sībyrhtes brōðor   and swīðe mæniġ ōþer
clufon cellod bord,   cēne hī weredon;
bærst bordes lærig,   and sēo byrne sang
285   gryrelēoða sum.   Þā æt gūðe slōh
Offa þone sælidan,   þæt hē on eorðan fēoll,
and ðær Gaddes mæġ   grund gesōhte.
Raðe wearð æt hilde   Offa forhēawen;
hē hæfde ðēah ġeforþod   þæt hē his frēan ġehēt,
290   swā hē bēotode ær   wið his bēahgifan
þæt hī sceoldon bēgen   on burh rīdan,

38

VIII. The End

The Saxon force fought fiercely,
grim spear-bearers, and bid of God
that they might avenge their kind lord
and deal death to their foes.
265   A hostage with them began to help.
Among the Northumbrians he was of courageous kin;
Ecglaf's son. His name was Æscferth,
and he would not flinch from battle-play
but sent forth arrows without fail-
270   sometimes found shield, sometimes men,
but always after awhile delivered some wound
for the time he could brandish battle-arms.
And there at the front, still standing, was Edward the tall
ready and willing, he railed boasting words,
275   that he would not forego a foot of land
or turn back now that Byrhtnoth lay dead.
He broke through shield-walls and fought the barbarians-
wreaked havoc on the Vikings; dealt vengeance
before he too was brought down on the battlefield.
280   Likewise fought Ætheric, a noble comrade,
bold and battle-ready, Sibyrht's brother-
he fought with earnest as those around him.
They split silver shields, and bravely defended themselves.
They smashed shield rims, and chain-mail sang
285   a terrible song. Then at length
Offa struck a norseman, felling him to the field-
and likewise did Gadd's cousin sink to the sweet earth,
for Offa soon was cut down in the fight,
though he fulfilled that promise,
290   the vow he delivered to the dear thane:
that they would ride together safe

hāle tō hāme, oððe on here crincgan,
on wælstōwe wundum sweltan;
hē læġ ðeġenlīċe ðēodne ġehende.
295 Ðā wearð borda gebræc. Brimmen wōdon,
gūðe ġegremode; gār oft þurhwōd
fæges feorhhūs. Forð þā ēode Wīstān,
þurstānes sunu, wið þās secgas feaht;
hē wæs on ġeþrange hyra þrēora bana,
300 ær him Wīgelines bearn on þām wæle læġe.
Þær wæs stīð ġemōt; stōdon fæste
wigan on ġewinne, wīgend cruncon,
wundum wēriġe. Wæl fēol on eorþan.
Ōswold and Ēadwold ealle hwīle,
305 bēgen þā gebrōþru, beornas trymedon,
hyra winemāgas wordon bædon
þæt hī þær æt ðearfe þolian sceoldon,
unwāclīce wæpna nēotan.
Byrhtwold maþelode, bord hafenode-
310 se wæs eald ġenēat- æsc ācwehte;
hē ful baldlīċe beornas lærde:
"Hige sceal þē heardra, heorte þē cēnre,
mōd sceal þē māre, þē ūre mæġen lytlað.
Hēr līð ūre ealdor eall forhēawen,
315 gōd on grēote. Ā mæġ gnornian
se ðe nū fram þīs wīġplegan wendan þenceð.
Iċ eom frōd fēores; fram iċ ne wille,
ac iċ mē be healfe mīnum hlāforde,
be swā lēofan men, licgan þenċe."
320 Swā hī Æþelgāres bearn ealle bylde,
Godrīċ tō gūþe. Oft hē gār forlēt,

40

in health to home, or perish here
on the war-field, dead from wounds.
His words were true as he now lay near his lord.
Shields crashed; the seamen advanced
fighting with fury. Spears found
fated men. Wistan then went forth,
Thurston's son, and fought the oarsmen,
and took down three in the throng
before he was hacked to the ground.
Fierce fighting was had; they stood fast
those soldiers in struggle. Warriors collapsed
wound-weary. The war-slain fell to the earth.
Oswold and Eadwold all the time
(both brothers) exhorting the brave,
their beloved cousins- bade them words
that in this desperate hour they must endure
and boldly wield their weapons.
Byrhtwold then spoke, raising his board-shield.
He was an old retainer, and shaking his spear
gave the battle-group bold counsel:
"Thought shall be the harder; heart the keener;
mood the more as our might lessens.
Here lies our lord now fallen,
this good man on the ground-- gives he his soul
who from this fight intends to turn.
My life runs its course-- from here I will not go,
but nearer my brave one's side,
beloved friend, I fight to the end."
So likewise did Godric give them heart-
Æthelgar's son- to the fight- he flung his lance,

295

300

305

310

315

320

wælspere windan   on þā wīcingas,
swā hē on þām folce   fyrmest ēode,
hēow and hynde,   oðþæt hē on hilde ġecranc.

325   Næs þæt nā se Godrīċ   þe ðā gūðe forbēah!

*   *   *

sent his spear into the Viking rank.
So he went forward first-
hewed and hacked the foe till he was felled.
325   He was not that Godric who gave up the field!

* * *

APPENDICES

A. INTRODUCTORY NOTES

1. Five versions of the *Anglo-Saxon Chronicle* are printed and translated in *Maldon AD 991*, ed. D. Scragg (1990).

2. See Alan Kennedy, 'Byrhtnoths Obits and Twelfth-Century Accounts of the Battle of Maldon', in *Maldon, 991*, ed. D. Scragg (1990), pgs. 59-78.

3. See Petty & Petty (1976), *Speculum* vol. 51 pgs. 435-446.

4. Lines 264-265 of text.

5. As line 90 states, landes tō fela (too much land) is given. Mitchell & Robinson (1992) suggest that the Vikings were playing on Byrhtnoth's overzealous defiance. Samouce (1963) suggests that Byrhtnoth may have let the Vikings cross due to the "ethics of the time."(134). Schwab (1993) associates the word *ofermode* with the attitude of a "proud warrior", and likens the word to the Middle High German *übermuot* (72).

6. See McKinnell (1975); Sklar (1975); Clark (1983); et al.

7. See Campbell (1993), in *The Battle of Maldon: Fiction and Fact*, ed. J. Cooper. Pgs. 1-17.

8. Ibid., 2-4.

9. The need (or custom) of a proper Christian burial may be emphasized here; see Griffiths (1991). The

significance of the German connection is a source of much debate. Woolf (1976) suggests that in a Christian society, such as tenth century England, the Germanic warrior code would not be a relevant concept. Griffiths (1991), however, points out that the Germanic ideal may not have been unknown in educated circles; thus, the author could have invoked its use (83). It is likely that the heroic ideal recounted in Tacitus' *Germania* and suggested by the *Maldon* author may have simply had a symbolic function-- a reminiscent ring for a people in transition.

10. The purpose of the poem, perhaps, engenders the most interesting debate that surrounds the poem. *The Battle of Maldon* should not be taken as a literal historical account of battle anymore than Tennyson's musings on the reckless charge of the Light Brigade, though such works are imaginative recollections of actual engagements. The possibility that the poem is a lament to the inability of the Saxons to effectively resist the Vikings (or Danegeld) is intriguing. It is fair to assume that some sort of heroic ideal is present in the poem, and that such an ideal can be applied to *any* community-- thus, the universal nature of Maldon's message transcends both politics and history.

B. NOTES ON TRANSLATION

Old English is a language that is a member of the Germanic branch of the Indo-European family of languages (a family of languages comprising most of the spoken tongues of Europe, India, and Southwest Asia). English itself has undergone many changes over the centuries, including the substantial infusion of French and Latin; thus, Old English is markedly different from the English language we know and speak today. Because *The Battle of Maldon* was written prior to the Norman conquest, the Saxon language of the poem bears a much closer resemblance to German, particularly in its variety of word order and inflected endings that indicate the function of the word. In addition, differences in sentence structures (for example, the splitting of subjects between verb and object, or the tendency to summarize with a pronoun or phrase a clause that had come before) lend to the difficulty of the language. Four dialects of Old English have been distinguished: Mercian, Kentish, Northumbrian, and West Saxon. West Saxon is the more prominent in written records, and the poem concerning Maldon is said to have been written in Late West Saxon.

As to the poetry, alliteration (the repetition of consonant or vowel sounds at the beginning of words) and stressed syllables within the line were very important in the composition of Old English poetry. Anglo-Saxon lines of poetry were generally divided into "half-lines", separated by a line break (or caesura). The pause at midline may have originated with the fact that poems in the oral tradition were accompanied by music, and the pause could have provided a space for a musical instrument. Each half-line in Old English verse could be stressed in five different ways, thus half-lines joined into single lines gave Old English verse a special intricacy. Stresses generally fell on the alliterated words, thus adding to the vigor of an Old English line's rhythm and pitch:

ex: "Folc and Foldan. Feallan sceolon"
(Line 54)

The initial letter of the first stress in the second half-line would have to alliterate with one of the stressed words in the first half-line (as above). Stress, however, was considered more important than alliteration. Rhyme, to which the modern reader is perhaps more accustomed, was not an important feature of Old English verse.

Because *The Battle of Maldon* was written near the end of the Old Anglo-Saxon literary period, the poem exhibits less of the rigidity of line present in earlier works. With the coming of the Normans, along with the propensity of versifiers to imitate French and Italian models, the counting of syllables and emphasis on rhyme and line-end gradually displaced Old English poetic form.

For this translation, I have attempted to keep true to the rhythm and alliteration of each line only where possible, in order not to sacrifice the sense or meaning of the words and lines ; therefore, I have not offered an exact verse reproduction. Where alliteration between half-lines was not desirable (due to lexical and stylistic constraints) internal rhymes and alliteration singular to individual half-lines were employed (cf. Lines 17-18, 204, 232, etc). The aim here was to preserve, or at least to suggest, the power and beauty of the music of the original while maintaining clarity of sense and textual lucidity.

C. MAP ILLUSTRATION

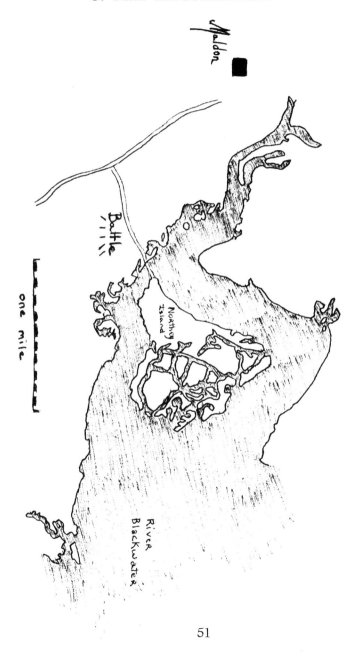

D. SELECTED BIBLIOGRAPHY

Alexander, Michael. *The Earliest English Poems.* 3rd ed. London: Penguin Books, 1991.

_____. *History of Old English Literature.* London: Macmillan; New York: Schocken, 1983.

Alexander, M., and Riddy, F.J. Eds. *The Macmillan Anthology of English Literature,* vol. I, *The Middle Ages.* London: Macmillan, 1989.

Campbell, James. "England, c. 991," in *The Battle of Maldon: Fiction and Fact,* pgs 1-17. Edited by Janet Cooper. London: The Hambledon Press, 1993.

_____, ed. *The Anglo-Saxons.* Oxford: Phaidon, 1982.

Churchill, Winston. *A History of the English Speaking Peoples,* vol. I, *The Birth of Britain.* London: Cassell & Co., 1956.

Clark, Cecily. "On Dating *The Battle of Maldon*: Certain evidence reviewed." *Nottingham Medieval Studies.* Vol. 27., pgs. 1-22., (1983).

Cooper, Janet., ed. *The Battle of Maldon: Fiction and Fact.* London: The Hambledon Press, 1993.

Finberg, H.P.R. *The Formation of England 550-1042.* London: Paladin, 1976.

Griffiths, Bill. *The Battle of Maldon: Text and Translation.* Middlesex: Anglo-Saxon Books, 1993.

Irving, E.B. Jr. "The Heroic Style in *The Battle of Maldon.*" *Studies in Philology.* Vol. 58., pgs 456-467., (1961).

Kennedy, Alan. "Byrhtnoth's Obits and Twelfth-Century Accounts of the Battle of Maldon." pgs. 59-62., in *The Battle of Maldon AD991.* Edited by Donald Scragg. Oxford: Oxford University Press, 1991.

McKinnell, John, "On the Date of *The Battle of Maldon.*" *Medium Ævum.* Vol. 44., pgs. 121-136., (1975).

Mitchell, Bruce., and Robinson, Fred., Eds. *A Guide To Old English.* 5th Edition. Oxford: Blackwell Publishers, 1992.

Petty, George., and Petty, Susan. "Geology and *The Battle of Maldon.*" *Speculum.* Vol. 51., pgs 435-446., (1976).

Samouce, W.A., "General Byrhtnoth." *Journal of English & Germanic Philology.* Vol. 62., pgs. 129-135., (1963).

Schwab, Ute., "*The Battle of Maldon:* A Memorial Poem." in *The Battle of Maldon: Fiction and Fact.*, pgs. 63-85. Edited by Janet Cooper. London: The Hambledon Press, 1993.

Scragg, Donald., ed. *The Battle of Maldon AD 991.* Oxford: Oxford University Press, 1991.

_____. ed. *The Battle of Maldon.* Manchester: Manchester University Press, 1981.

Sklar, E. S. "*The Battle of Maldon* and the Popular Tradition: Some rhymed formulas." *Philological Quarterly.* Vol. 54., pgs. 409-418., (1975).

Whitelock, Dorothy. *English Historical Documents,* Vol. I: *500-1042.* 2nd Edition. London: Eyre Methuen, 1972.

Wilson, David M. *The Anglo-Saxons.* Harmondsworth: Penguin Books, 1971.

Woolf, Rosemary. "The Ideal of men dying with their lord In the *Germania* and in *The Battle of Maldon.*" *Anglo-Saxon England.* Vol. 5., pgs. 63-81., (1976).

Samuel Salerno, Jr. was born in Nevada in 1965 and has lived his entire life on the Monterey Peninsula. After graduating from Pepperdine University with a B.A. in English, Mr. Salerno went on to receive an M.A. in Linguistics from the University of London in England. Mr. Salerno is also the author of two books of poetry: *Songs From the Sea* and *Noah's Ark*. He currently teaches History and English at the Robert Louis Stevenson School in Carmel, California.